Missing Pieces

by

Karen Mooney

First published 2022 by The Hedgehog Poetry Press

Published in the UK by
The Hedgehog Poetry Press
Coppack House, 5
Churchill Avenue
Clevedon
BS21 6QW

www.hedgehogpress.co.uk

ISBN: 1-913499-30-3

A CIP Catalogue record for this book is available from the British
Library.

For Stanley

Contents

SENT TO GRANNY'S FARM IN 1966

I helped her to feed the chickens
and collect the eggs each day;
observed her carefully buff them
before setting them like jewels
into cartons, stacked for collection.

If the shells were too thin
or didn't clean up well
they were used on the farm.
We got a boiled one for tea
with buttered wheaten farls
freshly made each day
on the griddle, the ingredients
measured in handfuls.

I remember coming home
from the farm, our house full
of big people dressed in suits
talking in whispers;
the empty carrycot in the corner.

CALCULUS

i.m. Joanne

Useless at maths, we struggled, rooted to the seat in fear, clamming up when questioned in class. You created a distraction, dividing attention, faking an asthma attack whilst we cheated. Taken away, until the teacher saw us laugh. Doubts set in with us, too, so we didn't pay attention to your undeveloped stature. We multiplied, raced ahead, leaving you gasping. It was our turn when your white coffin turned the corner.

Nothing added up.

PRE-PROGRAMMED

Wash day was well-rehearsed.
Gather clothes, sort colours from whites,
fill the Burco boiler, set temperature,
add washing powder, OMO or DAZ,
whichever was on offer.

Watch raw ham-like hands
rubbing fabrics together
in a programme set for each Monday
with starch-stiffened resolve
and a prayer for a good drying day.

Spinning hands to squeeze and wring
before an old mangle nipped fingers
if minds wandered -
dreaming of other settings.

BONFIRE

Dad drove us up the Rocky Road to see the bonfires lighting up a Belfast skyline. As a child, I didn't understand the significance but appreciated the spectacle and had no desire to go near them, nor would I have been allowed.

carnival for all
night sky illuminated
keep a safe distance

Years later, attracted by the excitement, I went to see one but perhaps it was just a chance to see a lad I had a notion of. Singing, dancing, a chaste kiss around the back of the boney; the fire was lit until my damper deployed with the thoughts of a disapproving father.

youthful excitement
drawn like a moth to a light
afraid of the fire

Dumped like the remnants that would not take to the flame, scarred like the bonfire site. I learned that several components were required for a real fire, that they should be handled with care and even more carefully set.

putting out the flames
charred to protect from danger
setting a new fire

Well, it doesn't mean that you're an arsonist if you light a few fires, and we're all long enough in the tooth to know that dying embers can be rekindled. But, mind you, sometimes those components have to be kept apart unless, of course, the hearth is empty and you need the heat.

hot ash can ignite
flicker or a flame, beware
playing with matches

A LITTLE BIT OF PARIS

No need of powder or paint lest it was Sunday
when Newcastle beckoned; canvas and tweeds
were replaced with polka dots, promenading,
Pierrots and possibility.

A Killarney honeymoon and trips to Scotland
formed the extent of her travels, but she kept
a little bit of Paris in her dressing table drawer,
close by the unused vanity set carefully placed
on embroidered linen doilies.

With a sweep of *Bourjois* rosette brune rouge
over crème puff, plumped cheeks,
she created a courageous canvas
held within a dignified frame.

She held it high, strode back and forth
to the local shops garbed in increasingly capacious
tweeds, all the while concealing the impact
of disability, five births and the loss of a child.

Cruelly betrayed, the frame hollowed out,
vibrant summer colour dulled to winter
as she carried the patina of malignancy.

REDUCTION

unique provenance   well-seasoned   concentrated
on high heat   lid off   simmering   reduced
yet packed   with flavour   smacking   of life's
experiences   just a small   portion   now
it doesn't go far   the   spread   across
the plate   curtailed   condensed   by
life   age   ill health   distilled
to   extracts of what matters
creating a memorable
aftertaste leaving
us wanting
more

VEGETABLE SOUP

We worked in silence using her recipe;
brought the shin bone to the boil
drained the fat off;
in went barley, lentils and split peas.

Dad suggested that we use
the pressure cooker.
Back up to the boil as we washed
and chopped, then added the vegetables.
We waited.
I was glad that he peeled the onions,
I didn't want to cry in front of him.

He tried to release the pressure.
The soup-stained ceiling was evidence
that he was in unfamiliar territory.
The little that was left tasted good.
Mum asked for seconds; I felt her approval.

Later, he told me that the doctor
had said that was how it would go,
something tasty whetting her appetite.

I hadn't realised that we had just
prepared her last supper.

PREPARED

Her clothes hung musty, in a wardrobe
long after the smell of perfume had faded.
Remnants of her life; boxes of baby tags,
old photographs to which we now turn.
On top, a savings book, insurance policy
and grave papers for a child not spoken of;
to whom she was preparing to return.

IN SEARCH OF THE RIGHT NOTE

You sang *One day at a time*
every day like a prayer
until the music stopped.
Now we live it,
singing out of key.

MY BEST FRIEND

He bought you the record,
dropped the needle on it
for Don Williams to sing
what he couldn't say;
lost his bearings
when troubled winds
searched you both out.
Adrift, he dropped
anchor at the roots of
your past until
he, too, could sail home.

LILY OF THE VALLEY

Shy, content in the protective shade,
reluctant to step into the limelight;
it hid under the skirts of the hedge
the way we clung to hers.

Planted when they moved there,
an alien city landscape, contrasting
with the freedom of her farm upbringing,
from where her rhizome roots renewed.

She walked down the aisle with it
after the fashion icon of the times,
Princess Grace, who, at the age of fifty-two,
died tragically before her time.

Two things they had in common.

OYSTER CATCHERS IN MARCH

He preens in a salty bath
from beak to claw,
trembling tail feathers
reflecting his mood.
She looks the other way,
having quietly taken note
that irrespective of plans afoot,
there's not enough heat
to raise a brood.

NEXT GENERATION

A sanguinary struggle;
bled out, no future, pain rife.

Not considered a loss at all
back then, just part of life.
Glad to be over it, back to work
sharp - like a knife, cutting routine
into segments, separating issues,
in control, emotions buried,
disposed of.

Until

you consider your role,
femininity, ability, the future
that nature stole.

No names chosen,
so less personal then?
Sure, at twenty-three
you can always try again.

Now, I wonder,
was I not then bereft,
or numbed into silence
now voiced by lessening years left?

No consideration,
no contemplation;
my justice, hope; miscarried
with my next generation.

WANING GIBBOUS

It's just a phase, you say,
withdrawing, hump faced,
darkening my nights,
leaving me to turn in,
to find my own light.

I, too, can change,
rid out negativity,
throw open windows,
clean, clear and sage
the corners to let go
of fear; knowing
that someday soon,
I'll meet the new you.

ROSE, IN WINTER

Walking through the Rose Garden
at Mount Stewart after a storm,
the bareheaded display of fragility
reminds me of how I once felt.
No one else will want you.
My illness had impacted on us
despite efforts to blossom.

Once tightly wrapped, bud-like,
my scent released only to you.
But as I started to open,
you became anxious, controlling,
perhaps losing trust. My petals,
gathered by you in furious gusts.

And in submission, I fold; retreat,
strength sapped, cut down to size
with a stare; cold.

But now I stand. I stand naked,
defiant as you lash my bones
with a cruel tongue that howls of gloom.

I will find another summer.
I will bloom.

OUR FUNERAL

There were no flowers or cards of condolence
yet there was a death, the death of us.
No handshakes, no wake or funeral service,
just fear that it may be contagious.

Likening the situation to death,
you envied the sympathy
for a neighbour's last breath
whilst I, suffocating, needed to be free.

Our union had become like a tether,
unlike a joining where two become one;
independence may have kept us together,
to complement, not complete: too young.

Black's not my colour, so I did not yield
to mourning openly but cried inside;
I wore independence like a warrior's shield,
protecting the land where failure resides.

Yes, we died, we buried our remains
in new lives, so our history we resist,
but no matter how deep the grave we dig
the bones of our past can be found to exist.

BREAKING OUT

Incarcerated behind
tightly drum-snared steel,
I hear the sun weep.
Staccato drenching timbre
releasing tension
as she smiles.

BEGINNINGS

so it ends
yet what follows
has not begun

possibility exists
in the spaces
between

as life stirs
in the belly
of winter

UNSPOKEN

Old rotten cloths
hang in that damp
musty room that
cannot be aired.

Pegged tightly
many years ago,
heat, condensation,
decaying inside.

Windows steamed up,
jammed or locked,
keeping intruders out
and regrets within.

A CLOSE SHAVE

I smile at the buzz of the electric razor,
knowing that you like to be clean-shaven;
feeling proud of having pieced it together
after you cast it across the table, declaring it *fucked*.
Until I catch your stare. This cuts deep.

Anything mechanical intrigued you,
rarely defeated you
but today, you wear exasperation
like a dry shave with a blunt blade.

Lessening dexterity thwarted once skilled tools,
your hands. Hands that could carry hold, lift,
repair, protect and even attack; shovel-like
and calloused now soft with lessening use.

Your attitude would soften too, in time.
But now, as your grip on the day lessened,
you bristled against it, so I applied the balm,
moving in the direction of growth.

Flipping open the casing on the shaver,
I flick out a spring, close it over,
check that it is silent and say
Yes, dad, you're right. It's fucked.

LAST RITES

The world would come crashing in around us
in as many days as it took to make
when you return to the care home, conscious
of our presence, attending your own wake.
You perform a rehearsal one evening;
we gasp at what we think is your last breath
then you rally to sit up, eyes gleaming,
ordering breakfast - your last before death.
One by one, folk call in to pay respects,
sit in silence or give a knowing nod.
You aren't fit to speak, yet touch does affect,
as one lady proved and how I applaud
her cradling your face in pillow-soft breasts;
prompting memories, you smile, feeling blessed.

LIFE-LONG LEARNING

The craft was engrained within huge calloused hands, their whorls, valleys and ridges blackened to reveal his unique identity. These hands were tools, trained to service engines in Harry Ferguson's; they worked on motorbikes, cars, lawnmowers and tractors. Toughened with each new project, restoring old cars and bikes, they conducted an orchestra of screaming valves in his domain at the end of our garden.

A flick of the lights from the kitchen signalled tea was ready, and the hands were rubbed on an oily rag before sweeping back *Bryll*-creamed hair. He would arrive in navy oil-stained overalls, the smell of grease, oil and petrol overpowering any remaining traces of the *Old Spice* aftershave applied earlier to temporarily scrub off his DNA with *Swarfega* in the kitchen sink before refuelling. Then, on a cold winter's night, he would bring his 'work' home. The engine would be laid upon newspapers in the living room. Whilst he worked his magic, we sat enthralled.

The hands would soften, as did he, yet it seemed that oil still coursed through his veins. He would read about engines, talk about them and listen to them.

Sadly, his own could not be restored.

the apprentice
masters his craft at eighty-four
time served

CARE, COURTESY AND CONSIDERATION

preparing to move
mirror, signal, manoeuvre
proceed with caution

I can still recall my brain inflated like tyres with braking distances, speed limits, road signs and markings long before any lesson. Commentating on my father's driving and passing *his* highway code test was a prerequisite before applying for a provisional licence. A mechanic to trade, the workings of the engine were, to him, of equal importance. So, I learned to change gear by listening to the engine revs, dip for oil, check the radiator for water, and change a wheel. Oh, and put petrol in, a condition of use.

He taught me to drive at speed whilst dividing the road into zones of visibility and invisibility when I'd *give her the guttie* or slow down. Clutch control was honed by moving at a walking pace behind a herd of cows whilst reversing was practised lapping the back field. Dad was a man's man, an alpha male widower left to raise a young family with no idea of preparing a teenage daughter for what lay ahead. I can see now that his tuition travelled beyond driving. I embraced it all with enthusiasm knowing that the keys of his car would liberate me, but what eighteen-year-old girl would be fussed about lying on the ground to check underneath a vehicle? This was Northern Ireland in the early eighties; dad was a policeman. I still close my eyes when I turn the key in the ignition.

BROKEN

I found you this morning,
all folded up, tucked in
at the back of my mind's drawer,
the one marked *do not open.*

Perhaps, it wasn't closed
tightly enough, overfilled,
contents ready to spill
if touched by hoping.

You appeared in jewellery boxes,
cards, photos, concert tickets;
in a souvenir mug that cannot be
held, its handle - long since broken.

RESTLESS MIND

What I wouldn't give
for just a penny's worth
of understanding at 4 am
to settle a restless mind.

I roll into that dip in the bed
trusting that you will be there,
drawing in the remaining scent
on the shirt, you left behind.

It's fading now, like scars
from the cuts of departure,
cleansed then by my tears,
yet they still fall in my mind.

DWELLING PLACE

A flowery idyll tended by a favourite brother of Mum's. The oldest male, who, by tradition, should have inherited the farm. He was relegated by health to this small roadside corner cottage to make room for a wife and family for his younger brother. They never arrived.

It was here that he gathered the tales and yarns of locals, weaving them into stories, poems and songs for my mother and aunt to perform in local village halls. He drew water from a well and read by the light of an old oil lamp. Dragging his twisted limbs around the garden, he created a living canvas. He was the farmer here; the plants, his family, blended in a way that Monet would have been proud of.

displaced and alone
creating a new story
making memories

He passed; it passed to Mum. We enjoyed country summers helping local farmers bring in the hay. Cycling deserted roads and lanes, sampling her upbringing at Granny's table. Dad calmed more quickly in the country air. The garden had become overgrown since a temporary let had resulted in tenants who did not care for the delicate planting favoured by my uncle. I recall the sweep of the scythe, as sharp as my father's tongue, being swung to clear the way for our playground; a haystack. The new growth made a sweet soft landing and gave way in parts for vegetables and strawberries. This place is where she planned a future alongside the past.

retracing our roots
leave the city far behind
nostalgia dwells here

She passed; it passed to Dad. He fled here to renovate and repair. He planned that for the cottage too. He rebuilt and extended; it and himself; he worked here and retired here. The ground now gave way for founds upon which he would build an extension, a structure that gave him hope. The garden was primarily used as an open-air workshop as the outhouses were filled with parts and tools. Here, he held his own brand of Sunday service. His mates would gather on a Sunday morning and he, ever the host, proffered whiskey, poteen, with whatever was in the fridge. Consumed in a smoke-filled kitchen; garnished with yarns and craic. He was at ease here.

flee to safe haven
re-treat, re-group to rebuild
a new religion

He passed; it passed to the eldest son. When the primary wish lists had been dealt with, it was cleared out, memories dispensed, boxes of past allocated. Mine held a set of toenail clippers, my Sunday school bible, school reports, and tucked between the pages a tiepin that had belonged to my father. The blue enamel twinkled like his eyes once had; this would live on elsewhere. Rusting machinery and old cars, securely tethered by grassy tussocks, were liberated for the local scrap metal merchant as the history of place and tradition became an asset. We found out through the neighbours and the local press what was likely to become of it.

cutting all the ties
planning permission is sought
replacement dwelling

AUBRETIA

You spill out of pots and beds,
seed waves of blue.

Mum grew you too.
Cuttings from the family farm
softened our city borders as you
trickled onto the lawn.
I'd lift you up if I was on mowing duty,
emulating her protective nature.

When I first had a garden of my own,
carefree, unruly borders
echoed my delight in life.

Until uprooted, then heeled in
where statement plants
and concrete block wall
protected a sterile plot.

Now, I smile at your undemanding
yet wilful nature as you run unbridled
between the paving and red brick steps
at my back door. You complement
age-covered pots; even venture inside.

Unlike mum,
cut down after the first flush in early summer,
you bloom again.

KINTSUGI

For Stanley

Smashed on life's floor
our jagged edges
made handling difficult.

Confidence and strength drained
through the fractures, hairline cracks
and missing pieces.

Tenderly and courageously
we gathered the shards
of ourselves, repairing,
filling gaps with a lustre
to celebrate the transient
imperfect nature of life.

A marriage of elements,
handled with care;
creating a vessel of hope.

ACKNOWLEDGMENTS

Thanks are due to the following publications in which some of the poems, or versions of them, were first published: *A New Ulster, Dreich, Ethel Zine, Paragraph Planet, Fevers of the Mind, formercactus, Hedgehog Poetry Press, Poetry NI, The Heron Clan, Live Encounters Poetry & Writing* and *NVTV* (Northern Visions Television).

Special thanks to my husband, Stanley, friends and family; to Mark Davidson, Editor, Hedgehog Poetry Press for the opportunity to have these poems published and for his ongoing support and encouragement, also to Gaynor Kane and Lynda Tavakoli for encouragement, advice and support.

Thanks also to the Irish Writer's Centre for a mentoring bursary with Moyra Donaldson; Lisburn Writers, The Coven of Write Witches and Women Aloud NI.

KAREN MOONEY

Karen started writing poetry in 2016 and has been published in the USA, UK, and Ireland. Her work first appeared with Hedgehog Poetry Press in *The Road to Clevedon Pier*, and she co-authored *Penned In* with Gaynor Kane in 2020.

Follow her on Twitter @1karenmooney or Facebook @observationsbykaren.